30 Days of Power!

A Mental Detoxification, by speaking
Daily Affirmations meant to empower
your life!

Christian Scott Publishing

Contents

This book is not a very intricate read. Not a very deep, read at all. It is purposely written this way. It's meant to be as simple and plain as possible! It may also seem repetitive, but that too is deliberate. It's written with the intention of bringing YOU to the realization; YOU are a CHILD of GOD! YOU ARE SUCCESS, GREAT and POWERFUL!! It's time YOU LIVE LIKE IT! I want you to understand something. Speaking from your inner spirit aligning it with what you believe will create your reality! If you don't get anything from these affirmations, get the power of BELIEVING! The more you speak something repeatedly, and consistently, it becomes implanted in your mind, what's in your mind, comes out of your mouth, whatever that may be, positive or negative, THAT THING,

WILL SURELY come to pass. The key is to ONLY BELIEVE! Say that to yourself, not out loud, but with your mouth closed from your INNER BEING. From THAT PLACE say......... "ONLY BELIEVE" say it again "ONLY BELIEVE" ......it's amazing you can hear yourself without speaking aloud?! From THAT PLACE is where these daily affirmations should be spoken. Once YOU connect from within and realize the GOD in YOU, you will never remain in doubt or defeat again. Start your day with THANKS. Begin the very first 5-10 minutes of your day with a quiet meditation of just being grateful. Think of 5 things you're grateful for and thank GOD for those things FIRST! There is ALWAYS something to be thankful for. Get into the habit of communicating with GOD, FIRST and DAILY (if you don't already). You'll be surprised how this sets the tone of your day. After that's done, speak the daily affirmation and expect to HAVE A GREAT and BLESSED DAY! Let's go! 30 Days of Power!!!!

When YOU make the decision that you're fed up with being regular, when YOU are tired of living below, what your gut instinct is telling you, you deserve! When YOU want more than what someone else is giving you. When YOU know, YOUR dreams, and YOUR GIFT will provide a better life for you and your family. When YOU decide to acknowledge YOU ARE GREAT! ACT! MOVE! Move forward and go after whatever YOUR dreams and goals are! YOUR FIRST move is BELIEVE! HAVE FAITH IN GOD! When your faith is unwavering, unshakeable, and FREE OF DOUBT, YOU CANNOT LOSE! (Matthew 21:21). GOD didn't give us the spirit of fear! (2 Timothy 1:7) He gave us the spirit of courage and VICTORY! STOP pondering over all the reasons you can fail and ONLY BELIEVE IN YOUR WINNING!! Secondly, CHANGE YOUR THINKING!! Condition your mind to succeed!! ONLY think success, ONLY think of seeing YOUR dreams through to fruition!! Focus ONLY on using

YOUR GIFT that GOD put in YOU, tailored for YOU, designed specifically for YOUR GREATNESS! Everything YOU NEED IS INSIDE OF YOU! ONLY BELIEVE! YOU WIN! Flat out, point blank YOU WIN! ACT LIKE IT, LIVE LIKE IT, TALK LIKE IT!!! Last SPEAK INTO YOUR OWN LIFE! Speak YOUR triumph! Speak your reality, The POWER of LIFE and DEATH is in the tongue! (Proverbs 18:21) SPEAK IT! Speak your dreams, speak your success, and speak your change into existence! Speak it BOLD-LY, LOUDLY and with CONFIDENCE! KNOW it's coming to pass, because IT IS!! This is the first day of the rest of your life! These daily affirmations are the beginning of transforming your mind and increasing your FAITH to ONLY BELIEVE! These affirmations are to change how you think, to ONLY THINKING SUCCESS, and to SPEAK YOUR GREATNESS into your life. This is a 30-day mental detoxification! Walk in your authority! IT STARTS TODAY!! 30 DAYS OF POWER!! LET'S GO!!

Day 1:

GOD is with ME! Everything I do TO-DAY is successful every challenge is easy, and every obstacle is overcome. I cannot fail because GOD is with ME. I have supernatural success in ALL that I do today. Proverbs 16:3

Day 2

I believe I can do and have anything I can envision. I am wealthy and prosperous in every area of my life. TODAY I demand and receive every BLESSING that's due to me, and in return I will be a BLESSING to others. Proverbs 11:24-25

Day 3

TODAY I move forward toward my dreams and goals. TODAY I will do at least one thing that takes me closer to using my GOD given gift to increase the quality of life for my family, myself or anyone in need. I am a lender not a borrower. I am SUCCESS!

Deuteronomy 15:6

Day 4

There isn't anything or anyone who can stop my progress towards my goals and achievements. There is a path for ME! My steps are ordered, and the outcome is determined by GOD, so therefore I WIN! TODAY I walk in VICTORY! Psalms 119:133

Day 5

I have supernatural FAVOR! TODAY and everyday moving forward, I only operate in GOD'S SUPERNATURAL FAVOR! I have favor with EVERYONE I encounter! My favor and faith defeats failure! So therefore, I prosper ALWAYS! Exodus 33:17

The biggest obstacle, largest hurdle in the way of your success is YOU! YOU and how you're thinking! Only YOU can stop YOU! Success is inevitable, when you're determined, focus and ONLY BELIEVE!!! What's between your ears "YOUR BRAIN" is the ONLY object or thing that can stop you! There is nothing more you need, there isn't a special person you need to meet; there is no special day, time or hour that's set aside for your victory, your success, or your dreams. The time is NOW!!! That day is TODAY! RIGHT NOW!!! If you're struggling with the FACT that it starts TODAY? Ask yourself "WHY NOT"? Why can't it start TODAY? What will I lose? If you do ONE THING, take ONE step, a step that could begin to change the rest of your life for the BETTER, TODAY?! Why not?!

What would be wrong with that?! What's stopping you?! NOTHING! ABSOLUTELY NOTHING!!!! ANYTHING you imagine, ANYTHING you dream, ANYTHING you can envision, can become your REALITY!!!! Stop being content with average! Start thinking from your SUPERNATURAL MIND!!! With GOD ALL THINGS ARE POSSIBLE!! (Luke 1:37). You were made to be great!! GOD didn't intend for you to be average. CHANGE your thought process, ONLY BELIEVE! (Mark 11:14). EVERYDAY speak, declare, and pronounce your success! Stand on it! Believe it! These Daily affirmations are the beginning of strengthening your mental and spiritual muscle. They are meant to be read with CONVICTION, BELIEF, and AUTHORITY! YOU ARE SUCCESSFUL!!! The rest of your LIFE begins TODAY!!!! Your thoughts dictate what you speak! Unfortunately, for whatever reason, we think of what cannot happen more than we think of what CAN happen. How you envision LIFE, how you envision what you are capable of is EXACTLY what is going to show up in your life!! CHANGE YOUR THINKING, CHANGE YOUR WORDS! Get obsessed with success. Get obsessed with ONLY BELIEVING!! YOUR GIFT is YOUR LANE!!! GOD made it specifically for you!!! TAP INTO IT!! It's what makes you great! HOWEVER, IT ALL BEGINS with YOUR FAITH, THOUGHTS and WORDS!! TODAY IS THE DAY; YOU BEGIN TO MAKE YOUR DREAMS BELIEVE!! 30 DAYS OF POWER!!!!

Day 6

Everything I need to succeed is within me. GOD has built me for greatness! Today I operate within my greatness and towards my purpose. I am triumphant in the valleys, because I'm destined for the mountain tops. (1 Corinthians 3:16)

Day 7

Today I start fresh! Today I'm thankful and grateful for the air I breathe. Only today counts, yesterday is passed! Today I restart my life again! No worries, no stress of what tomorrow brings. My needs are met and provisions made for me, because I am covered by GOD! (Matthew 6:25-34)

Day 8

My words are the gateway to success. My mouth is the street to my abundance, what I speak creates the Avenue towards what I believe I am, and to what I believe I have. So today I speak overflowing blessings into my life, today I speak supernatural success in my work, and anything I am directly involved. Today I speak favor! Today I conquer ALL! Today I win, I win, I win, I win!! (Mark 11:22-24)

Day 9

Today I walk in forgiveness! I forgive everyone and anyone that I feel may have wronged me in anyway. Today I leave all drama behind and will no longer carry old hurt. I release myself from the baggage of the past pain and shed the spirit of anger. I forgive, I forgive, forgive. Today is the beginning of new relationships and I will walk in GOD'S LOVE! (Matthew 6:14-15)

Day 10

Today I operate fearlessly! Fear does not have a place in my life! My faith, anointing and GOD'S word cancel out fear. Today I boldly claim my increase, and my prosperity in every area of my life! I will walk in my GOD given authority form this day forward! So today I courageously, command the results of GOD'S blessings to manifest in my life in JESUS name!! (Deuteronomy 31:6)

It's only impossible until someone does it......It is only impossible until SOMEONE DOES IT!!! If you can imagine it, then you can achieve it! If you can see yourself doing it, if you can see yourself having it, if you can imagine YOU living in it, YOU CAN HAVE IT! It's already done! NOW GO GET IT!!! Snatch it out of the air in JESUS name! Proclaim it boldly! GO TO GOD BIG!!!! YOUR FAITH is the multiplier!!! Big as your FAITH, big as YOUR BLESSING! Understand YOU ARE NOT chasing success, YOU ARE SUCCESS!! Feed your mind with, what you want your life to be, and what you want in it! What you take in is what you get out!! Stay focused! Write down your vision, print out pictures of your vision and hang them up. YOU CAN and WILL DO IT! JUST GET MOVING! 30 Days of POWER!!! Let's Go!!!!!

Day 11

I CAN DO IT!!! There is nothing I can't conquer; there is nothing I cannot do! I will not give up! Nothing is impossible, GOD is with me, so ALL things are possible. I am GOD'S favorite child! So today I know I CAN DO IT and I WILL DO IT! (Philippians 4:13)

Day 12

I am in control of my thoughts, words and actions. I am in control of what and who I allow to occupy my space. What I choose to feed into my mind will ultimately affect my life. So TODAY I choose to only think positivity, abundance, prosperity, favor, and success! I am powerful. I am intelligent! I am a winner! I am great! I can't lose, I don't lose, and I won't lose, because GOD says I am BLESSED! (Philippians 4:8)

Day 13

What "THEY" say doesn't matter. Negative words from those against me, have no effect on my life. They do not and cannot change what GOD has for ME. I will not allow the opinions of others to distract my focus! TODAY I am moving forward! Their chatter doesn't matter. Only positivity is allowed in my space. Only GOD'S word stands!! (Proverbs 20:19)

Day 14

Where there is difficulty, I see possibility! Where there is pain, I see reward. What's behind me is the past. Today, I only see what's ahead! I won't turn around to look, I came through it! I beat it! I am a winner! Who can stop me?! NO ONE! I am victorious! (Romans 8:31)

Day 15

My blessings are plenty GOD is my supply. My potential is endless GOD is my supply. My needs are met GOD is my supply. My goals are surpassed GOD is my supply. My business is prosperous, GOD is my supply. I am anointed for success because GOD is my supply! My land, my properties, my assets are increased starting TODAY, because GOD IS MY SUPPLY!! (Deuteronomy 1:11)

Whatever your current situation is at this moment, whatever your circumstances are, whatever you're going through, DO NOT allow it to deter you from pursuing your dreams, and going after what you desire and deserve. I tend to believe that time is one of the greatest gifts GOD has given us. Time keeps moving, the earth keeps rotating, the sun rises, the sun sets, the night ushers in a NEW day, and it does and will get better! There isn't any bad situation that will last forever. Every day is a new day, another chance to start over. What A BLESSING!!!! It's not how many times you fall; it's how many times you get up! Every transformation, every rebuild, every change, requires a certain level of being uncomfortable. Get used to it! Invite it because you KNOW the change for the better is coming. Soreness precedes the muscle growth, demolition before the renovation! YOUR TIME IS COMING!! Briefly think about all you've overcome. When it looked like there was no way, when you thought you weren't going to make it through, YOU MADE IT!!!! YOU'RE HERE!!! YOU'RE STANDING! YOU'RE A WINNER! BELIEVE IT, because it's TRUE!!! Remember EVERYTHING IS POSSIBLE! YOU ALWAYS WIN! ONLY BELIEVE!!! 30 Days of Power! LET'S GO!!

Day 16

Circumstances are not my truth. Situations don't dictate where I end up. Bad positions can't hold me. The facts aren't MY TRUTH! Today MY TRUTH is, I am more than a conqueror! MY TRUTH is I am a lender and not the borrower! MY TRUTH is that, I am the righteousness of GOD! MY TRUTH is, anything I ask in the name of JESUS and believe for, I have ALREADY received it! MY TRUTH is that, I am heir to the promises of Abraham, Isaac and Jacob! Today I stand in MY TRUTH! (Matthew 22:16)

Day 17

The mistakes I've made don't define me. The mistakes I've made won't stop my success. In fact, each mistake was another block for me to stand on that raised me up a little higher each time. Each mistake was another rung on my ladder as I climb to the top! Today I am who I am from every single mistake. My mistakes have made me strong, wise, and given me the knowledge to succeed. Today I embrace everyone. Each one was a custom cut, a custom mark, just for ME in this diamond GOD gave me called LIFE! I am powerful, great, intelligent; successful……I am ME! (Psalms 139:14)

Day 18

What's for me is for me. What plans and ideas I have, I will keep to myself. I will speak with GOD in my quiet place. I will not allow any negativity to hinder my blessings, by speaking before it's time. Today I pray in secret as GOD will bless me openly. Today I move forward boldly, confidently, but in blessed silence toward my goals. My success will speak loudly! (Matthew 6:5-6)

Day 19

Prayer changes everything when you believe. Today I believe and pray, the correct doors will open, doors that were closed before, NOW, TODAY have opened for me. I pray GOD that you direct my steps; keep me on the path you've already chosen for me. I pray today, immediately, all interference, every obstacle is moved out of MY way in JESUS name! I pray GOD'S blessings over my life, the life of my family and anyone connected with me. My NEW LIFE starts TODAY I believe it! I pray that every idea, every business venture, every relationship, any and everything I am involved with is successful and prosperous! I pray increase over my territory. I am the righteousness of GOD! I decree, believe, receive and pray this TODAY in JESUS name! Amen! (Mark 11:23-24, John 15:16)

Day 20

Today I will shut my mind off to all distractions. I will purpose myself to be quiet, meditate, and listen from my spirit. Listen, so I can hear what GOD is instructing me to do, where GOD is instructing me to go, who GOD instructs me to connect with and GOD'S plan for my destiny. What GOD puts in place for me, is greater than anything I could want or do for myself, and greater than what I could ever imagine for myself. Starting today, I get out of my own way, and will allow GOD to dictate my success. What GOD gives me; no man can take away! Today I open myself up to receive what GOD HAS FOR ME! (1 Corinthians 2:9)

TRUST IN GOD! Your increase, your position, your favor come from GOD! Even though the assignment, the acknowledgement is given through, MAN, the APPOINTING is from GOD! The POSITION is from GOD! What GOD has for you no one can take away, PERIOD!! TRUST THAT! No matter where you are right NOW, KNOW, this is not your last stop, YOU ARE PURPOSED for MORE! DO IT!! Don't be afraid of what MAN says, don't get discouraged, when they can't see your vision, or they won't believe in you. That's when your faith comes into play, that's when you rely solely on what you know in your spirit, your heart and your mind and you ONLY BELIEVE! Don't be afraid to fail, failure brings VICTORY!!! Failure sets you up for the VICTORY!! History, has it that Colonel Sanders, the founder of KFC was turned down a record 1,009 times! Picture that!! He heard the word "NO" 1,009 times when trying to sell his recipe for fried chicken. Get this! It wasn't until he was 65 years old and wasn't satisfied with the amount of the social security check he was receiving, that he decided to sell his delicious recipe driving around the country going DOOR TO DOOR. The one thing he didn't do was quit! HE NEVER QUIT! HE NEVER STOPPED BELIEVING! Imagine if he would have given up, if all the people that turned him down, all 1,009 of them, would have caused him to stop believing, there wouldn't be a KFC today. He DID NOT allow MAN to stop his greatness. He didn't even start until he was 65 YEARS OLD!! Failure is temporary, VICTORY is permanent!! Failure can only become permanent if YOU QUIT. In every sport there is a Champion, no matter what happened before, no matter how many losses, you can never take away that CHAMPIONSHIP! They did it! He won! Whether it was 1000 losses or 10,000 losses that CHAMPION-SHIP will last forever!! FOCUS on winning and ONLY BELIEVE! Believe in what GOD can do, believe in where GOD can take you, and believe in what GOD says! Remember FAILURE IS TEMPORARY, VICTORY IS PERMANENT!!

Day 21

It doesn't matter how much I hear the word "No" I will ONLY BELIEVE. "No" doesn't mean I stop, "No" doesn't mean I give up, "No" doesn't mean I've failed. It only means THAT situation wasn't the one for ME. THAT person wasn't the one to connect with. THAT wasn't the one GOD chose. "No" has "no" effect on my success. One hundred "No's" mean NOTHING to "ONE YES"! Today I decree my "YES"! Today I ONLY BELIEVE, GOD'S YES! (2 Corinthians 1:20-21)

Day 22

It's nothing wrong with dreaming BIG. My dreams are the preview of what's to come in my life. If I BELIEVE it, SPEAK it; THINK it, then I WILL HAVE IT! Today I begin to dream bigger, today I speak my dreams into existence! In CHRIST my dreams will manifest in my life! In my dreams I am great! In my dreams I am prosperous! In my dreams I am a blessing to others! My DREAMS are the trailer to my REALITY! Today I BELIEVE IN MY DREAMS! (Genesis 15:1)

Day 23

The ability to give is one of the greatest gifts I have, to give to someone in need, to give to someone out of the kindness of my heart, to give myself, my time or something, that could change someone else's day, situation, or life is a choice rather than circumstance! Giving creates the passageway to receive. I don't need to have a whole lot of any ONE thing to be able to give a little bit of SOMETHING. Today I will begin to give those very things I believe to receive! Today I will give cheerfully, willingly, and wisely! Today I will give from what I lack to create space to receive my abundance. (Luke 6:38)

Day 24

THANK YOU! Today I am THANKFUL! I thank GOD for allowing me to have the GIFT of TODAY. I'm thankful for every minute. Every moment, every hour, every second, I have, is proof of GOD'S grace. I am grateful! I'm thankful for every problem, thankful for every blessing, thankful for having what I DO have. Thankful for my victories and thankful for my failures, GOD kept me! Thankful I'm not where I could be, and grateful for where I am! Grateful for the gift of imagination, and thankful for what I know and believe is yet to come! LIFE alone is a gift and I'm THANKFUL for every day I get to LIVE it! (1 Thessalonians 5:18)

Day 25

I WON'T LET GO!! I won't let go of my dreams! I won't let go of my business plans; I won't let go of GOD'S promises for my life! I won't let go of my mission for success! I won't let go! I won't let go of my ideas, my plans, my desires for myself and my family! I won't let go! I won't let go of the hope I have for my prosperity, my relationships, my marriage, my career! I won't let go! Today every plan, imagination, and desire I have put out of my mind and allowed circumstances to cause me to lose focus, I put back into effect today! I won't let go!!! (Genesis 32:26-29)

Day 26

I have no limits! There are no limits to where I can go, what I can do, what I can have, or what I can achieve. There are no limits to my success, my dreams or imaginations. The only person that can stand in my way is ME! I control how far and where I go, I determine my level of success, I am my only barrier! Today I recognize, I am exceptional, and I was made to be great! Today I begin to operate and live with no limits! With GOD I have no limits, no boundaries, and I can conquer anything! I BELIEVE IN ME! With GOD I AM LIMITLESS! (Psalms 147:5)

Day 27

GOD is BIG! There is nothing small about GOD! He is infinite! How BIG my blessings can be is determined by how BIG GOD is to ME. How large my imagination is, how BIG my belief is, how wide my thoughts are will determine the size of my territory. Think small, get small, think BIG receive BIG! GOD wants to bless me HUGE! Today I increase my faith, Today I increase my belief, cast out my unbelief and dream BIGGER than I did yesterday! Today I believe BIG, Today I expect BIG, Today I command BIG, because GOD made ME to live large!!! (Deuteronomy 28:11)

Day 28

NOTHING IS IMPOSSIBLE!! It's only impossible until someone does it! Everything is POSSIBLE! There is nothing I cannot accomplish! There is nothing I cannot overcome! There is nothing I cannot have. There is nowhere I cannot go! ALL THINGS ARE POSSIBLE! Today I ONLY BELIEVE it's ALL POSSIBLE! Whatever I can imagine, think or see, in MY MIND, CAN BE DONE!! My success is POSSIBLE, my DREAMS are POSSIBLE! IT'S ONLY IMPOSSIBLE UNTIL SOMEBODY DOES IT! Today I vow to DO THE IMPOSSIBLE! (Luke 18:27)

Day 29

Ⅰ am POWERFUL! I was born POWER-
FUL! My strength, my courage, my wis-
dom, my greatness already exists, INSIDE
OF ME!! I already have EVERYTHING I
NEED to succeed! I am unstoppable! My
vision is the car, my imagination is the en-
gine, my dreams are the wheels and my
BELIEF/FAITH are the keys! Today I start
driving down the roads of prosperity, the
streets of success, the blocks of blessings,
and the Avenues of abundance! Whatever
I THINK, I AM! Whatever I say, I HAVE!!
GOD loves ME! I am HIS CHILD, and I
AM POWERFUL! (Timothy 1:7)

Day 30

Today!!!! I AM made WHOLE!! Everything I ever lost is restored! I am PROSPEROUS! Every broken relationship is mended! In EVERY area of my life there is abundance! The impossible is possible for me! GOD lives in ME! I have no limits!! GOD LIVES IN ME! There are no barriers! GOD LIVE IS ME! I will stand at the top of the mountain because I SAID IT, I SEE IT, I KNOW IT, I BELIEVE IT, and because GOD LIVES IN ME! My resurgence begins today!! (Joel 2:25-26)

Expect the miraculous EVERYDAY! Everyday expect your breakthrough, wake up with the thought TODAY is my outbreak! Remember the feeling you had as a child, the days before Christmas? That's the feeling you should purpose yourself to have. GOD has already done it, know this in your heart, and believe it in your soul! Speak it, speak it, and speak it! Every day is another opportunity for you to EXPECT BIG! Say this …. TODAY, is the day of miraculous change in my life!! Say it again and again, until it becomes cemented in your heart, mind and every thought you have! Remember "as a man thinketh, in his heart he is" (Proverbs 23:7). Change your thoughts, speech and actions; YOU CHANGE YOUR LIFE!

******30 DAYS OF POWER!!*****

Made in the USA
Coppell, TX
21 September 2022